HOW TO SERVE A PROPER

VICTORIAN TEA

Using Antique China and Silver
to Bring the Past to the Present

CAROLE PICHNEY
P.O. Box 944
Bayport, NY 11705

Published by Carole Pichney, P.O. Box 944, Bayport, New York
11705 (516) 472-9395.

ISBN 1-57502-306-7

Library of Congress Catalog Card Number: 96-97051
Second Edition

Printed in the USA by

*M*ORRIS
PUBLISHING

3212 E. Hwy 30
Kearney, NE 68847
800-650-7888

~Acknowledgements~

I would like to thank the following people for their help with this book: my husband Dan Pichney for his patience and support; Frank DeRubeis for all his computer expertise and saving the day many times; Andrew DeRubeis for his illustrations; Judi Culbertson for inspiration and support; Jane Pettigrew for her knowledgeable comments on this book; Ellen Easton for all of her invaluable advice about publishing this book; Nan Guzzetta for costuming me and helping me buy my tea set; Pam Raymond and the late Kaye Magale for helping me with my very first tea; Marion Cohn, Ann Marie Roberts, Jeanne Carlsson, Jan North and Terry Lerch for sharing their knowledge of silver and antiques; Jane Raven and Marlene Goldman for their wonderful recipes; and the librarians of Suffolk County for their support and encouragement.

I would especially like to thank Michele DeRubeis for her many long hours of work on this book, her research and patience in putting it together. Without Michele there would be no book and I thank her more than words can say.

"The kettle was always on in my house growing up... whether it was a simple cup of tea to start the day or our traditional Christmas afternoon tea with my grandmother's homemade mince pies with all the trimmings from Yorkshire. Today, the ritual can be just as simple or as elaborate as time and a special occasion allow.

"I applaud Carole Pichney's efforts in sharing her historical research, beautiful presentation and her warm enthusiasm for *Having Tea*."

Trish Foley, Author, *Having Tea*
    Contributing Editor, *Victoria* Magazine

~ Table of Contents ~

~ Foreward ~

I had the pleasure of meeting the author of this delightful book at a tea conference held in Connecticut earlier this year.

Carole Pichney, the author of *How to Serve a Proper Victorian Tea*, has been living her book for several years now - she serves Victorian teas and gives lectures at libraries, museums, historical societies, charitable events and churches. Carole's Victorian Tea presentations are enthusiastically embraced by her audience. Recently, she has been asked by the Jane Austen Society of North America in New York City to make presentations about how tea was served in Jane Austen's day, and during the Colonial period. Carole dresses in full Victoriana and delights in using the antique silver tea accoutrements when serving her audience.

How to Serve a Victorian Tea is a very practical book. Carole shares with her readers the joys of tea, the places local to her residence (Long Island) where you can enjoy tea, and buy tea, and the things to accompany your tea.

The historical parts of the book are entertaining, educational and accurate (the author has certainly done all her homework!). A good sprinkling of personal information is also included which balances out the plethora of information nicely. Carole has high standards for serving tea, and it shows in her book - she advocates the use of loose tea (as I do), and discusses the everyday uses of tea strainers, mote spoons, sugar tongs and lemon forks. Her chapters have catchy, and cautionary, titles, such as *Use Cozies Carefully!* and *Take the Pot to the Kettle, Never the Opposite* and goes on to explain the reasoning, an instruction George Orwell agrees on in the sixth point in his essay *A nice cup of tea.*

Possibly the best way to read *How to Serve a Proper Victorian Tea* is to imagine Mrs. Pichney speaking to you about the delights of taking tea, interspersed with historical tidbits, while serving you (white gloved) on the front porch of her restored 1873 Victorian house, on Long Island, with her antique silver tea service, scones, clotted cream, preserves and two types of tea. What makes this book so appealing is its steady flow of accurate information, combined with a personal tone.

How to Serve a Proper Victorian Tea can be carefully studied, or used to take a light quick dip into fashionable tea jargon. Whatever the use, this is a delightful treasury, with wonderful tidbits of information.

Melody Wren, Publisher, Editor,
  The Charms of Tea Newsletter,
  Guelph, Ontario, Canada

~ Preface ~

In March of 1993, I gave my first presentation of *How to Serve a Proper Victorian Tea* at the Sayville Inn in Sayville, Long Island. Since that time time I have spoken to thousands of people on Long Island at libraries, museums, historical societies, charitable events, churches and other places about serving loose tea, properly, in the Victorian manner. Recently, I gave a presentation to the Jane Austen Society of North America about tea in Jane Austen's time at Mohonk Mountain House, a perfectly preserved Victorian Hotel in New Paltz, New York. In the near future, I will be giving a presentation on Colonial period teas for the Van Cortlandt House Museum in New York City. I have also been asked to present in several other states. What began as a local presentation in the New York area has now spread throughout the United States thanks to readers of the first edition of my book and their friends. In this second edition, I have included readers' suggestions as to where you can enjoy special afternoon teas and catalogs where you can order tea to be shipped anywhere. I urge you to contact me at the address in this book to make additional suggestions to share with fellow tea lovers.

In an article Eileen Swift wrote about me in *Newsday* in June of 1993, she said I was out to create a "tea renaissance". At the time, I thought that rather amusing as it was not my intent. I find, however, three years later, that Eileen was right after all.

Everywhere I have spoken to people about Victorian teas, they have embraced the subject with great enthusiasm. Among friends, having tea has become a regular part of our lives. Collecting tea pots, silver tea

3

strainers, and sharing new blends of tea has united us in friendship.

As president of the Bayport Heritage Association helping to restore Meadow Croft, the summer estate of President Theodore Roosevelt's cousin, John Ellis Roosevelt, in Sayville, Long Island, I have had the opportunity to have many teas there. Our annual "First Bloom Tea in the Antique Rose Garden" has been a joy to this community. We gather on a Friday evening in mid June for high tea and to stop and enjoy the roses which we would otherwise never find the time to do at that very busy weekend of the year when so much else in happening in our lives. This exemplifies what is so appealing about a renaissance of teas. Our lives are so very busy that we do not take time out for the beauty of nature and of sharing friendship and simple pleasures. It is time for a change; I think we all feel that way. Taking time for tea is a simple way of making this change.

This book is meant to share with you the joys of tea and the places where you can enjoy tea and buy tea, clotted cream and the things you need to accompany your tea. I hope you will use this book and enjoy reading it as much as I enjoyed writing it.

~1~

Use Loose Tea, Never Tea Bags

If you want to serve a proper Victorian Tea, you must never use tea bags. Tea bags were not even invented until 1904, three years after Queen Victoria died in 1901.

The use of loose tea gives you infinite variety and choice in the types of teas you can use. As you will discover when you begin drinking teas, it is almost like appreciating fine wines. There are many different types of tea for morning, afternoon, and evening. Like wines, some are fruity; others bold and distinctive. Teas are affected by the soil they are grown in, the altitude of the place they are grown, and the sunshine and rain conditions of that particular growing season. A second flush Darjeeling, meaning the second growth of that season for the tea plant, can be extremely fine and delicate; a Lapsang Souchong can be bold and smoky.

It is fun to taste different types of teas and different flushes or growths of the same tea. The very finest teas are only available in loose tea and it is possible to buy very small quantities of loose tea so that you can try many varieties with relatively little expense. You can then buy larger quantities of those you like. Look for the growing number of stores in your area that are selling loose tea and speak with the owner for recommendations.

Have a tea tasting party for your friends. Let them try several varieties, but try to choose varieties that are distinctive so that they can taste the differences fairly readily. Also limit the number of teas to 5 or 6. As you all become more knowledgeable and sophisticated in your appreciation of teas, you can introduce greater subtleties. For a first time tea tasting you might have English Breakfast Tea, Green Gunpowder, Lapsang Souchong, Darjeeling, and Earl Grey. Most of all have fun with it! Do not make it too serious or stuffy. I gave a 70th birthday tea for my mother. Her friends later confessed to me that they were afraid it was going to be "stuffy" and too formal and they were intimidated. As it turned out, they had the most wonderful time and later organized a 40th Anniversary Tea for their church. They dressed in Victorian costumes, had someone play period music on the piano, and had a member dress as Queen Victoria who gave prizes for the best costumes. One woman told me she had not had this much fun in 30 years!

The popularity of Jane Austen of late has had her books flying off the shelves of our public libraries. I recently organized a slide show for the New York Chapter of the Jane Austen Society of North America, and have offered it to the many libraries I work with here on Long Island. I am happy to say that "literary teas" are now being introduced in our libraries. Liz Burns of the Cutchogue Library asked for my scone recipe so that she could make it for her book discussion group on Jane Austen. I emphasize once again that these teas should not be stuffy or too serious. Have fun with them, as Jane Austen and her friends would have.

When you use loose tea, the ritual of brewing it becomes a ceremony and involves specialized things that are not necessary when you brew tea using a tea bag.

A **tea caddy** is necessary to hold the loose tea. When tea was introduced in Europe in the sixteenth century, tea was shipped from China in large containers. Tea was very expensive and valuable and was sold in small quantities. Tea caddies, whose name was derived from the Malay word kati, meaning a weight of aproximately 1 to 1.5 pounds, were necessary. At first, tea caddies had only one compartment to hold tea. As tea drinking became more popular, two compartments were added so that hostesses could serve both black and green tea. Later, they added a glass mixing jar to fit within the caddy so that the two types of teas could be blended to the taste of the hostess and guests. The earliest tea caddies looked like medicine jars and were quite small. As the caddy evolved, it was made of wood, silver, china, or other materials. It is fun to collect tea caddies when you search for antiques or even rediscover the antiques within your own family. Katherine Stevens has an antique store in Huntington, Long Island with a very large selection of tea caddies. In addition to the ones in the store, she has others not on view that she will show you if you ask.

Tea Caddy

I urge you to speak with older relatives as they may have tea equippage packed away that no one has been interested in for many years. They will be thrilled to share it with you and see you enjoy it as they once did. Share a cup of tea with them also; it will bring you both more pleasure than you can ever know. A wonderful book, *A Cup of Christmas Tea*, tells a beautiful story about how a young man became reacquainted with his great aunt and the memories of his childhood.

Tea caddies had locks on them because the tea in them was so valuable. Their owners carried the key on a chain around their necks so that the servants would not steal the valuable tea. In fact, tea was so expensive that tea leaves were often reused. They were dried, and even stained so that they appeared fresh and new. Such illegal tea became a problem and also evaded the tea import taxes. In Victorian times, the cook was entitled to the scraps and waste from her kitchen and the used tea leaves were considered her property to reuse or sell.

Caddy spoons are spoons with short handles so that they can be left in the tea caddy. They are used to convey the tea from the tea caddy to a warmed teapot. Caddy spoons were first introduced around 1760. Often they are in the shape of shells, as a shell was included in the earliest boxes of tea as a measure. As silver became more and more popular, especially during the Victorian era, caddy spoons became extraordinarily diverse and fanciful. They are relatively common today both in England and the United States and are fun to collect. They are fairly inexpensive, and fun to use in your "proper" tea service.

Mote spoons also are used to convey the tea from the caddy to the teapot. Mote spoons are much more rare than caddy spoons. In fact, I had searched for one here on Long Island for a long time and was not able to find one. When I made a trip to England to do research for my presentations, I was determined to find one. I scoured antique shops in London and Bath in search of a mote spoon. When in Bath, a shop owner told me "they are as rare as hens' teeth" and suggested my greatest chance of finding one might be in the Silver Vaults of London. What I did not know was that mote spoons were only made between approximately 1700 and 1780. They predated the tea strainer which began to be used in England around 1900. On my very last day in England, along with my friend Marion Cohn who had visited the silver vaults on her honeymoon, I found my mote spoon. I did not bargain on the price, but was thrilled with the beautiful spoon I now possessed. I could not wait to get home and brew a pot of tea to use it. My George II mote spoon was made in 1755.

The mote spoon served several functions. First, like the caddy spoon, it conveyed the tea from the caddy to the teapot. What makes the mote spoon different from the caddy spoon is that the bowl is pierced so that the "dust" from the loose tea can be sifted from the whole tea leaves that make the best tea. It is ironic that this "dust" is what is used in tea bags today. That is because it is fine and fits in the little tea bags and also because it brews instantly and we do not have to wait the requisite brewing time that fine teas require to develop their flavor. Just one or two dunks and the tea is ready for drinking. The mote spoon also had two other functions. Its long pointed end was used to clear the tea spout of tea leaves, and it was also used to skim the top of the tea for motes or floating "spots" of tea. Remember, when the mote spoon was first used, the tea strainer was not yet

9

invented, so that tea was poured directly into the teacup. Tea leaves would have come through the spout and were then skimmed off the surface with the mote spoon.

Do not confuse the mote spoon with a sugar sifter. Sugar sifters are quite common and before I had slides to show people the differences between the two, many people thought they had mote spoons. Sugar sifters, used to sprinkle powdered sugar onto desserts, do not have the point on the end of the handle. That is a distinctive difference.

Because of their scarcity, mote spoons are also one of the most counterfeited of all antique silver pieces. The price for an authentic mote spoon is probably not less than $200. I urge people to investigate their family silver to see if there is a mote spoon there. People are now scouring yard sales on Long Island for mote spoons.

The dating of English silver, although initially very intimidating, is really quite simple once you know the codes. The English marking system for sterling employs four symbols. The first mark is the city mark. The symbol for silver items made in London is the leopard's head. There are different marks for different cities of manufacture in England, Ireland, and Scotland. The second mark is the purity mark. The third mark is the maker's mark and the fourth mark is the date mark.

With not too much trouble and a good guide book you can learn to date your silver pieces and find the maker and city of manufacture. A good guide book is *Pocket Edition, Jackson's Hallmarks, English. Scottish, Irish Silver and Gold Marks* by Ian Pickford available at local bookstores.

A magnifying glass or jeweler's loop might be necessary if the marks are very small. They are usually on the back of knives, forks, and spoons and on the bottom of silver tea services. The reason that they are on the back, is that when the marking system was started, tables were set in the French manner where the bowls of the spoons and tines of the forks were set facing toward the table, the opposite of the way we set tables now in the United States and in England. It was around 1750 that the bowls of the spoons were turned toward the diner. The French table service to this day retains the opposite placement.

Have fun looking up the marks on your old silver pieces or ask an antique dealer to help you.

Caddy spoon

Mote spoon

12

~ 2 ~

Use Fresh Boiling Water

It is imperative that you use fresh, boiling water to brew your tea. Here on Long Island and in New York City, we have some of the finest tasting water anywhere. It is not necessary to use bottled water to brew an excellent cup of tea. However, in California, some southern states, and other parts of the country, the water may have a high mineral content or odor of sulfur or chlorine. If you do not like the taste of your water, use bottled water. People tell me that the tea purchased in England never tastes the same as it does here in the United States. It is probably because the water there tastes different.

On my first trip to London, I went to Fortnum and Mason, an English institution that has been "grocers and provision merchants" to the British aristocracy for over three hundred years. The store clerks there still dress in tails and it is quite an experience to visit and have tea there. I met with the tea buyer and manager, Mr. E. P. Hayes, who told me that if I brought 2 liters of freshly drawn water with me when I returned to England, he would blend a tea for me especially designed to complement the taste of my water here on Long Island. On my next trip, I lugged the requisite 2 liters in my carry on bag in the airplane and took them to him the first morning I was in London, so that the water would be as fresh as possible. To my severe disappointment, he told me that I needed twice as much water as I had brought, due to the many trials he would need for blending. He also said I could mail the water to him, which I have never quite gotten around to doing. At Fortnum and Mason you can buy their New York blend of tea which has been made especially to be brewed with New York City water. Unfortunately, you can only buy it in London, so make sure to stock up on it when you are there.

When boiling water for tea, it is important that you do not let the water boil for a long time as this will deplete the oxygen from the water. The notion of a whistling tea kettle may seem nostalgic, but to get the best tasting cup of tea, you should use the water just as it comes to the boil.

The hot water is necessary to have the tea leaves reach their full expansion. An exception to this rule is when brewing green tea. Due to the delicate nature of this tea, the tea water should not be allowed to boil, but should be poured on the tea leaves right before it reaches a boil.

Tea Kettle

~3~

Hot the Pot

When brewing tea properly, it it always necessary to hot the pot before you put in the tea and the boiling water. By placing a small amount of water in the teapot from the kettle before it comes to the boil, you can warm the teapot so that it will take as little heat as possible from the brewing tea. By using water just before it comes to the boil, you can be sure that when the water does boil, you are able to use it right away without having the oxygen boil out of the water.

People often ask me what type of teapot to use. Some people swear that tea can only be made properly in a china pot. I use my beautiful Victorian silver tea service all of the time and find the tea tastes wonderful from it. People tell me often at my presentations that the tea I make is the best that they have ever tasted. I think that the beauty of the silver tea service adds to the joy of taking tea and thus enhances the flavor.

I have a special red clay teapot which I only use for green tea. If you are going to use a porous pot of this type you should have a separate one for black, green, and flavored teas as the pottery will absorb the flavors.

I encourage you to collect and enjoy teapots of all types and materials. Use them in different table settings, different seasons of the year, and for different types of teas. One of my favorite teapots is

15

a replica of Monet's teapot which he designed for use at his home in Giverny. I like to have tea in the garden on a beautiful summer afternoon as the women in many impressionist paintings did. This teapot, designed around the turn of the century, looks extremely sleek and modern. It is, in fact, older than many of the Victorian looking teapots in my collection. Friends have often told me that I should not keep that teapot in my china cabinet that holds all of my special tea equippage because it looks too modern. Only after you have been to Monet's home and gardens in Giverny, France can you understand how he designed it to go with the colors of the rooms of that house and the paintings in it.

Every time I use Monet's teapot, I am transported back to my visit to Giverny and to those gardens of the 1890's. I bought the teapot at the gift shop at Giverny. The woman who sold it to me was a volunteer from the United States who came to Giverny every summer to work at the museum. The pot was quite expensive and I did not know if I could spend that much money on one teapot. She encouraged my extravagance, "So many teapots, so little time". She told me that her daughters begged her to bring them a piece of the china each time she came from France. I have blocked from my memory how much I paid for that teapot, probably around $175 to $200 dollars. I carried it on my lap in the plane and have treasured it ever since. On my last trip to France I wanted to get the teacup and saucer for the set. This china has become very popular in France now and the cup and saucer alone were over $100. I did not buy one.

Tea became extraordinarily popular both in the United States and England beginning around 1850. It is said that the popularity of afternoon tea had a great impact on the proliferation of the silver industry. As the custom became more and more popular, the demand for silver tea sets and other tea equippage increased dramatically.

Prior to the nineteenth century, silver was very expensive, but ironically not as expensive as the tea brewed in it. Before the 1860's, coin silver was the silver used in making silver items. Coins, usually from Mexico and Peru, were melted down to obtain silver. In 1859, the Comstock Lode was discovered in Nevada and other mines were opened in the Western United States which made domestic silver cheaper and more available.

In England, the process of electroplating was discovered in 1840. This made silver items much less expensive and more available to the growing middle class. Victorians enjoyed new foods such as oysters, asparagus, and sardines, in addition to afternoon tea, and wanted silver pieces designed especially for these new foods. Our progressive dinner group in Bayport recently designed a dinner around this type of specialty silverware. We had Oysters Rockefeller, poached salmon with dill sauce and capers, mango sorbet and cream of carrot soup because we had the Victorian silver and china to serve these dishes. Many of the items had never been used by one of the group members before as she had recently inherited them. It was an extraordinary dinner.

During the early nineteenth century, many silversmiths were located in southern New England. As the process of silversmithing went from hand hammered silver to manufactured pieces during the 1850's, large silver plants were opened there.

Of particular interest to me is the Meriden Britannia Company of Meriden, Connecticut founded in 1852. By 1856, it employed 74 people; and within a few

17

years it had 320 employees. This company manufactured a large amount of silver plated items. As president of the Bayport Heritage Association, I am working with the Suffolk County Parks Department, the Roosevelt family and others to restore Meadow Croft, the former summer home of President Theodore Roosevelt's cousin John Ellis Roosevelt in Sayville, New York.

One rainy afternoon when Philippa Roosevelt (wife of Philip James Roosevelt who is the grandson of John Ellis), came by rather unexpectedly to show an out-of-town guest the estate, I had the opportunity to ask her what had happened to the tea set from Meadow Croft. Somehow even when other furniture disappears, grand pianos and silver tea sets always are treasured. She knew nothing about the silver tea set. I showed her an inventory of all of the silver purchased for Meadow Croft in the years 1891 and 1892. We are very fortunate that these inventories were preserved by the Theodore Roosevelt Association in Oyster Bay. She had never seen the inventory and I immediately gave her a copy. It listed among other silver items: teapot $7.05, sugar pot $4.50, and two other items for $4.95 and $4.50 whose names could not be deciphered by the typist transcribing the ledger from the Meriden Britannia Company. I would assume that one of the items was a creamer; the other may have been a tray or trivet. A short time later, I received a phone call from Mrs. Roosevelt stating that she had located the tea set! She said she found it in a box with other items labeled "Sayville". Sure enough it was marked Meriden Britannia on the bottom. She was sure this was the set.

The family had left Meadow Croft by 1939 and only visited there once a year for a birthday picnic for John Ellis' daughter Jean Roosevelt. Mrs. Roosevelt said that we could serve tea from the tea set at our historical society holiday open house and I made arrangements to go to her home in Oyster Bay to pick it up. When I arrived there, she showed me several other beautiful silver pieces from the family including a child's silver bowl inscribed "Pansy". Pansy was one of the three daughters of John and Nanny Roosevelt.

The tea set was unusual to me. It was rather simple, the plating was worn from years of polishing, but most distinctive was heavily repoussed flowers which looked like sunflowers or chrysanthemums. I thought this very unusual and very different from the Victorian silver I had seen. Since beginning to research this teapot, I learned that American wildflowers were a theme for silver at this period. I thought it an extremely appropriate pattern for Meadow Croft, a country estate established to enjoy nature by a family very interested in the conservation movement. In addition to Theodore Roosevelt and his affection for the Teddy Bear and support for a national parks system, John Ellis Roosevelt's father, Robert Barnwell Roosevelt, was a pioneer conservationist who wrote many of the first fish conservation laws in New York State and was the first Fish Commissioner.

I am happy to say that I have just completed my research on the tea set. While vacationing and researching tea in Miami Beach, I attended a show at the Wolfsonian Museum. There were several interesting teapots in the show which led me to want to know more about the teapots in the Wolfsonian collection. I was able to make arrangements to use the research library for an afternoon during my trip and was helped by Pedro Figueredo to begin my research on the Roosevelt tea set. Pedro had worked in the library of the New York Historical Society and knew that there were catalogs from the Meriden

19

Britannia Silver Company on microfiche there. When I returned to New York, I called the New York Historical Society who told me that they had some of the trade books in their library and they were from a Dover publication. I also contacted the Meriden Historical Society in Meriden, Connecticut. They told me if I could tell them the pattern number of the set, they might be able to help me. In the meantime, they sent me a drawing of the set they thought it was from my description. Unfortunately, it was not the set.

I called Mrs. Roosevelt and asked her to draw the silver markings on the bottom of the set and any numbers that might be on it. I planned to send this to the Museum or take it into New York City to the New York Historical Society. I then remembered that it might be in a Dover publication, and the research librarian at the Patchogue Library was able to help me find the book. Fortunately, it was still in print and I ordered it from my local book shop. It took over a month for it to come, and when I first went through it I did not see the tea set. I was crushed. I went through every tea set in the book and could not find it. It was only a week later that, in going through the entire catalog leisurely, did I find it before the section on tea sets. I was so thrilled! I found the pattern number Mrs. Roosevelt had drawn for me 1972 and sure enough it matched! What an experience it was for me to be holding the very same catalog that Nanny Roosevelt had ordered that tea set from in 1891. The tea set will return to Meadow Croft when it is furnished as a museum. I hope that someday we can have a tearoom there, as other museums do. It would certainly be the perfect setting to enjoy afternoon tea.

~ 4 ~
Take the Pot to the Kettle,
Never the Opposite

Take the teapot to the kettle in the kitchen if necessary; never bring the kettle to the teapot in another room. The reason for this is that once again we want to ensure that the tea water is as close to boiling as possible when it meets the tea leaves.

I have heard people say that the water loses one degree per second, but I am not sure that has a scientific basis. In England and the United States during the Victorian period, kitchens were purposely located far from the drawing rooms where tea might have been taken. If you had to bring the tea kettle all of the way from the kitchen, it would be losing heat all of that time. Furthermore, you would be showing off your old tea kettle with your beautiful silver.

I am fortunate that my beautiful Victorian tea set has a kettle with a spirit burner as part of the set. This allows me to boil water in my parlour as I prepare the tea, so I do not have to go to the kitchen with my teapot. When I first purchased my tea set and wanted to use the alcohol burner, I found it had no wick. I went to the old fashioned hardware store in town hoping that he would have the proper sized wick. He told me that all the wicks that he had were too large for the opening in my alcohol burner. He suggested that I find an all cotton shoe lace and that would probably be about the right size. Sure enough, I went home and took one of the laces from a pair of shoes and it fit perfectly. I filled the well with denatured alcohol and let the wick soak up the alcohol for a short time. I then lit it with a match and it worked perfectly. Since then I never throw out the shoe laces when I get a new pair of walking shoes.

In the early days of silver manufacture, complete tea sets were not made. People would buy a silver teapot; and perhaps later on, the sugar bowl and creamer in the same pattern or a different pattern. It was only later that entire sets were made. During the Victorian era, tête-à-têtes, which were 3 piece tea sets (teapot, sugar, and creamer), were made in addition to sets which could include a teapot, coffee pot, sugar bowl, cream jug, slop bowl, tongs, tea strainer, kettle and tray.

I acquired my own tea set at the Pier Antiques Show in New York City which I attended with my friend and costume expert Nan Guzzetta from Port Jefferson, Long Island. I was determined that I was not going to make any purchases that day, unless I found the

22

perfect silver tea set. To my surprise, there it was, the exact one I had always wanted. Nan thought I should buy a different one because she felt it had more value as an antique; but I had my heart set on the one I eventually bought. Nan was nervous and thought that I should call my husband before spending so much money. I said I didn't have to and Nan negotiated the sale with the provision that I could return the set if I did not like it. We lugged that heavy silver tea service from the Pier Show to the parking lot several blocks away, all the time trying to hide it so that we would not be mugged.

I never returned the tea set, and have used that set at countless teas, parties, and presentations. It has been a constant companion. When I first bought it I thought it would remain in a box because it would be so hard to clean, but Nan told me to try Goddards's Silver Cloth. I have used that cloth ever since, and I am amazed at how long the set can go without polishing. It never went into a box and remains on the sideboard in my parlour.

Nan has just opened her dream shop in a mansion she purchased in Port Jefferson, Long Island. Ever since I have known Nan, she talked about the mansion she would one day buy for her clothing, furniture and prop collection. Her dream is now a reality and she has separate rooms for her Tudor, Victorian, 18th Century and twenties collections. Being at Nan's is a cross between being in a costume museum and a place for adults to play "dress up". I have watched many people arrive and try on costumes in Nan's shop. The minute they put on the costume they assume the character they are dressed as. It is pure magic and fantasy. You should try dressing up in period clothing as one the most wonderful ways to transport yourself to another era. If you haven't seen the movie *Somewhere in Time*, you should get

~5~

Separate the Leaves From the Tea After 3-5 Minutes

Separate the tea leaves from the tea after they have brewed for three to five minutes. After you have hotted the pot, discarded that water, measured one scant teaspoon of loose tea per cup, added the freshly boiling water to the teapot, and let the tea brew for the requisite time, you must strain the tea or it will become bitter and very strong. Ideally, you should just make one cup of tea for each person you are serving; strain it directly into their cups, and make a new pot of tea for the second serving. Therefore, if you are serving two people, it is best to have a two cup teapot, for four or six people, a teapot of that number of cups. If you do have extra tea after a cup has been poured for each person, it is very important that you strain it into another warmed teapot. You can then cover that pot with a **tea cozy**, which we will discuss in more depth in the next chapter.

Often, I have tea alone in a tearoom or hotel where I am sampling the tea service. I am usually served a large pot of tea which after five minutes or so begins to get strong and bitter. When I ask for more tea, they simply add more water. That is usually my test of a good tea service. When I ask for more tea, new tea leaves and fresh boiling water should be put into the teapot without having to ask. Now, however, I am very explicit when I ask for more tea. I ask for fresh tea leaves and boiling water.

25

Last summer, I spent time in France researching the French version of afternoon tea. At the Mariage Frères tearoom in Paris, I was taught the art of French tea making. I was surprised that the French are more careful about tea making than are the English. At Mariage Frères, a cotton "tea sock" is used to brew the tea and then is removed so that the tea will not get bitter. Please see the chapter on "Tea in France" for a full description of tea brewing using the the sock.

~6~

Use Cozies Carefully!

Use cozies carefully! This is one of the most controversial areas in my presentations. Criticizing the beautiful, innocent little tea cozy is like speaking against motherhood and apple pie! How could anything so charming and appealing cause any trouble at all? I tell my listeners that they can use cozies correctly if they separate the tea leaves from the tea as we discussed in Chapter 5. If the leaves are taken from the pot or the tea is strained and transferred to a warmed pot , then it is perfectly fine to put the cozy on the pot to keep it warm. To leave the tea stewing with the tea leaves in it and the cozy on, makes for a hot, bitter cup of tea.

People from England and Ireland tell me that their mothers never separated the leaves and always used cozies. All I can tell them is if they want the finest cup of tea, not bitter or "stewed", they should brew the tea properly.

My friend Linda Schwartz from Northport, Long Island has several beautiful antique tea cozies. She bought one when we were on a Christmas house tour in Setauket. I know she uses them and loves them, but I am not sure she always follows my advice.

Tea cozies come in all shapes and sizes. My friend Joan Courtney has a beautiful Irish knit tea cozy that looks like an Irish fisherman's sweater. She always uses it at her St. Patrick's day party.

Tea cozies are fun to collect. You can even have them custom made in the shape of your house. Just remember, use caution.

Tea Cozy

7

Offer Sugar Cubes with Tongs, Lemon Slices with a Lemon Fork and Milk (Never Cream)

Using the proper tea equippage is part of the fun of serving a Victorian Tea. This is what makes it different from other types of entertaining and creates the ritual and style of the tea. Sugar must be served with **sugar tongs.** Sugar tongs are relatively inexpensive. You can often find them between five and ten dollars at yard sales and antique stores. Sugar tongs were first made in the 1770's.

Sugar cubes, rather than granulated sugar, must be used or how can you say, "one lump or two?" When I entertain, I like to use brown lump sugar that is rough and not cut evenly into cubes. This is because sugar used to come in a cone and was cut off for use in sweetening. I have pictures from the eighteenth century that show sugar that looks exactly like the kind of brown lump sugar you can buy in gourmet stores. It is not inexpensive, but it lasts a long time and it really adds a nice touch to your tea party. I like the fact that it is not bleached. I am not sure when they started bleaching sugar; that will be part of my later research.

Sugar nips can also be used, but they were from an earlier period. Victorian women would have considered them an antique. I discovered sugar nips in my quest for a mote spoon. Sugar nips are like sugar tongs except that they have a scissor-like handle mechanism. They were first made in the eighteenth century and are more common than mote spoons. My sugar nips date from 1760 and the maker was John Perry. The marks are on the inside of the shell at the tip of the nips.

Lemon slices should be offered to your guests for a proper tea. Use a pretty dish. I have an antique lemon slice dish with a little handle on it that I acquired many years ago at a historical society antique shop. I always use it for lemon slices and enjoy seeing it on my tea table. Queen Victoria popularized the custom of drinking tea with lemon. She brought the custom back from Russia where her daughter was the Princess Royal.

When you serve milk with tea, make sure you never use cream. Even though custom says cream and sugar, cream has too high a fat content and the tannin in the tea tends to react with the cream.

While we are on the subject of cream, I always offer **clotted cream** at my Victorian tea parties. People unfamiliar with clotted cream ask if it should be put into the tea. I take it for granted they know that it goes on the scones with jam or preserves. Once people get a taste of clotted cream, they are hooked on it. I have seen the most diet conscious women heap clotted cream onto their scones. It is not low in calories or cholesterol, but it is one of the most delightful treats on earth.

Clotted cream comes from England. It is sometimes called Devon cream after that dairy region in England. I always buy it in little jars imported from England. Some local sources here on Long Island are the Quiet Corner Cafe in Port Jefferson, Wild by Nature in Setauket, and La Bonne Quiche in Northport. People ask me what it is. I tell them it is cream that is cooked over very low heat for quite a while. I do not

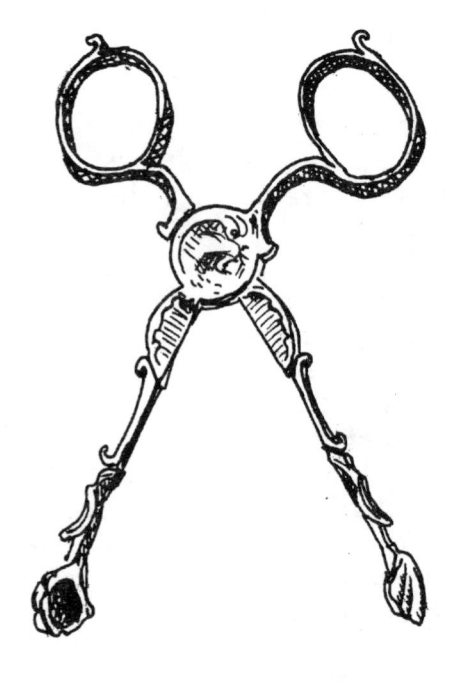

Sugar tongs   **Sugar nips**

know if the cream they use in England is homogenized and if that makes the difference. My friend Kaye Magale who did a great deal of cooking for Bayport Heritage Association and other local charities made clotted cream once for me for one of the first tea presentations I did. I don't know how she did it, but it came out great. I tried it once, and found so much waste it was not worth the effort. I also worry about cooking things over such low heat. I advise you to buy it. It keeps a really long time in the refrigerator and tastes wonderful.

On my tea research trip in England, Marion Cohn and I had the "terrible" job of having tea every day at a different elegant hotel or tearoom. Every afternoon I would taste the clotted cream and say "this is the best clotted cream I have ever tasted". And the next day I would taste the cream and say the same thing. They were all slightly different, coming from different cows from different regions, but they were all exceptionally good. People often substitute whipped cream for clotted cream. As far as I am concerned, this is not an acceptable substitute. I judge a tea by the quality of the clotted cream.

𝔓ut the 𝔐ilk in the 𝔠up 𝔅efore the 𝔗ea

𝔓ut the milk in the cup before the tea. There is a very practical reason for this rule.

When the British people saw the fine porcelain bowls from China that arrived as cargo with the tea, they had never seen anything so fine before and were afraid that boiling tea would shatter the porcelain. So, they poured in a little milk first to reduce the temperature of the tea.

Another reason for putting the milk in the cup first is that it prevents you from overfilling the cup. If the tea is put in the cup first, there may not be enough room left for the milk.

Use Bone China Cups and Saucers, Preferably Antique, and at Least One Piece of Vintage Linen

Bone china teacups or other china cups are necessary to serve a proper Victorian tea. Never serve tea from paper cups or especially Styrofoam. When I give presentations at libraries, museums, and historical societies, I always ask ladies to bring their own special teacup. The historical basis for this was that in the early eighteenth century, china teacups were so rare and valuable that people carried their own teacups with them in little boxes when they went out for tea. In fact, teacups were so valuable that the lady of the house would not permit her servants to wash the teacups. She personally washed each cup to ensure it was not broken. The practical reason for bringing china teacups is that paper or Styrofoam would be used as most groups hosting a tea presentation do not have a supply of china teacups.

Women love bringing their special teacups, and often have stories to share about them. At my presentations, we leave time to tell about the teacups people have brought. There are many stories about grandmothers, great grandmothers, aunts, and godmothers entrusting them with their precious teacups. It seems that many people skip a generation when it comes to interest in antiques. That is, a daughter might not be interested in her mother's china, but a granddaughter or great granddaughter often is.

34

Garage sales on Long Island seem to be a wonderful source of teacups. Women love telling about the bargains they got on their magnificent teacups. At one of my presentations recently, a woman brought two teacups she had gotten from her grandmother. They were from the Red Rose Tea Company. She did not realize that the objects on the outside of the cup, a horseshoe, wishbone and a flower were outlined in tea leaves. The cup, I told her, had symbols used in tea leaf reading. Sure enough, we turned over the cup and on the bottom it said "Cup of Fortune". This led to a lively discussion among the group about tea leaf reading. They are now off to buy tea leaf reading books and discover a whole new area of fun.

In all the groups I speak to, rarely do two women ever have the same cup at a meeting. There is an infinite variety of teacups and the fun of serving in them is that they are all different. You do not need a matching service of teacups. It is much more fun to use different cups. Let people choose the teacups they want, and you can tell stories about how you acquired the cups. It is a great conversation starter.

The cups do not have to be bone china. Bone china was first made by J. Spode in the eighteenth century. Indeed, bone ash is mixed into the clay; and England is the only country that produces bone china. Bone china is thin and translucent and keeps tea very hot. I like to collect bone china cups with pictures of the flowers in my garden. It is such fun to sit with my trillium cup when the trillium are in bloom in our wildflower garden. I also have a lily-of-the-valley cup, in addition to all the seasonal flowers from roses to chrysanthemums.

My friend Jean Carlsson collects Staffordshire china. This is not truly china, but earthenware. It is very

35

beautiful and much of it is Flow Blue. The history of Flow Blue and the blue willow china is fascinating; but it will be covered in my tea book about Jane Austen, which reflects tea service in the eighteenth century.

Jean has a beautiful collection of Staffordshire which includes cups and saucers, platters, serving dishes and dinner plates. Jean has taught me about how this transferware is made. This china was one of the first forms of mass produced china. The process entailed engraving a design deeply into a metal plate, usually copper, which was used like a stencil. China was hand painted in earlier periods.

Vintage linen is also necessary for a "proper" Victorian tea. While it is nice to use cloth napkins when you serve tea, it is not necessary to do so if you really do not want to wash and iron all of those napkins. You should, however, have a vintage tea cloth, or place mats or some type of linen. The workmanship on antique pieces is very different from anything produced commercially today. I am very lucky to have a table cloth from my grandmother, one of the few family pieces that I have. When I first found it in my mother's linen closet, it was very yellow and stained. I was amazed at how beautiful it came when I bleached and starched it. My friend Carol Weinhardt first showed me the effect bleaching had on vintage linens. I was really afraid to use bleach as I felt it might destroy the fabric. She helped me to bleach a vintage slip that we acquired for virtually nothing because it was so badly stained and yellowed that no one wanted it. I could not believe how beautiful it came after we carefully bleached it.

Trisha Foley, author, stylist, and a contributing editor of *Victoria* magazine, in one her books, *Linens and Lace,* gives very complete details on the care of vintage linens. I would urge you to read this beautiful book. Trisha also wrote a wonderful book on tea, and has been very instrumental in helping us to restore the house at Meadow Croft. She has shot several *Victoria* magazine layouts at Meadow Croft and each time she has done so she has prepared the paint and plaster so that the room can be decorated later according to our plan for the museum. She has been a tremendous supporter of our project and almost always includes a tea service in her photos. We thank Trish, Nancy Lindemeyer, editor in chief of *Victoria* magazine, and all of the staff for their help. There is a wonderful story in the July, 1995 issue about a fantasy Edwardian weekend at Meadow Croft. Of course, I had to buy the tea set used in the shoot.

~10~

Use a Pretty Tea Strainer with a Saucer, or a Mote Spoon and a Slop Bowl for Waste Tea

Tea strainers, in all varieties, shapes and sizes add to the ambiance of the tea. As discussed previously in Chapter 1, tea strainers were first used in England around the turn of the century. They were used earlier in Holland. The larger punch strainers were in use earlier in England to strain oranges and lemons when making punch.

Strainers can be sterling silver, plate, brass or other metals. They can have their own saucers or be put over slop bowls. A friend of mine who lives in Chinatown in New York City tells me that bamboo strainers are used by the Chinese as they feel that metal affects the taste of the tea, especially the delicate green tea.

Strainers can also be of porcelain or china. These look lovely over a bone china cup. It is fun to hunt for tea strainers in antique shops, flea markets, and yard sales. Here in my own neighborhood where I have been giving tea presentations over the last few years, I find it is virtually impossible to find tea strainers in local shops as so many people are collecting them. I know they are using them and enjoying them, but I wish they would leave a few for me.

Mote spoons, antiques for the Victorians, can also be used if you are lucky enough to have one. I am thinking of forming the "Mote Spoon Society" of Long Island. People who own mote spoons, or can borrow one from a friend, can get together to enjoy tea and compare their rare possessions.

Slop bowls are absolutely necessary if you are going to serve loose tea. This is a very ugly name for a very beautiful silver or china bowl. The purpose of the slop bowl is to have a place to discard the loose tea leaves that have gathered in the strainer and to have a place to rest the strainer to catch the dripping tea if the strainer does not have a saucer of its own. It is also a place to discard cold tea from your cup if you wish a fresh cup of tea, or do not like the type of tea that has been poured.

You are very lucky if your tea set has a slop bowl. The reason I bought my silver and china tea sets was because they both contained slop bowls. I bought my china tea set at Don and Carol Weinhardt's yard sale when they were moving to Massachusetts from Bayport. The only reason I bought Carol's tea set was because it had the slop bowl.

If you do not have a slop bowl, another bowl will do. Look for one with high, straight sides, as opposed to one that is shaped like a soup bowl. This shape will serve to hide the "dregs" from tea cups.

Remember, you do not have to have a full formal tea set to start enjoying tea. A nice teapot, a china cup, a strainer, sugar cubes, tongs, and a slop bowl are all that are necessary. Do not let having a matching set or the money to purchase expensive items stop you from serving tea properly. Enjoy loose tea now, and add to your collection as you go along. Remember, drink tea, properly. It is one of the simple pleasures of life that can return you to a period of elegance and style, qualities that are often missing in our busy lives today.

Tea strainer

A Proper Victorian Afternoon Tea

Cucumber Sandwiches on White Bread*
Egg and Cress Sandwiches on Whole Wheat Bread

~ ~ ~

Scones* with Strawberry Preserves and Clotted
Cream

~ ~ ~

Lemon Curd Tarts*, Victorian Poppy Seed Cake*

~ ~ ~

Several Varieties of Loose Tea

~ ~ ~

Sherry, if desired

*Recipes may be found on the following pages.

JANE'S CUCUMBER SANDWICHES

3 large cucumbers
2 large packages (8 ounces each) of Philadelphia
   Cream Cheese, SOFTENED
salt
1 small onion
Large Loaf of Arnold's or Pepperidge Farm White
   Bread

Peel cucumbers and cut off both ends. Cut in half lengthwise. Scoop out all of the seeds with a spoon. Now cut each half into quarters lengthwise. Put the long cucumber strips together and dice into pieces about 1/4 inch long.

Place the cucumber pieces into a colander and salt them lightly, stirring to make sure all of the pieces are salted. Let sit in the colander for at least one hour so that the moisture can drain out of them. **This is a critical step and must not be skipped or the cucumber sandwiches will lack flavor and the filling will be watery.**

After they have drained for 60 minutes, stir the cucumber pieces into the softened cream cheese. Stir until the cucumbers are coated. Grate a small onion into the mixture to your taste.

Assemble several slices of white bread on a cutting board. Put the cucumber filling on each of the slices, being careful not to put the filling all the way to the edges as the crusts will be cut off. Put tops on all of the slices. Cut off the crusts and then cut each sandwich into thirds. Stack on a platter with plastic wrap between the layers. Cover with plastic wrap so that the platter is air tight and refrigerate until serving time.

RASPBERRY'S TEA SCONES

2 cups all-purpose flour
3 teaspoons baking powder
1/4 teaspoon salt
1/3 cup sugar
4 tablespoons cold, unsalted butter
1/2 cup currants or raisins (optional)
1/2 cup sour cream
approximately 1/2 cup of milk
1 egg
2 teaspoons sugar

Preheat oven to 375 degrees. In Cuisinart, or mixing bowl, sift flour, baking powder, salt, and sugar. Cut in butter until mixture resembles coarse meal. Add raisins, mix in sour cream, and enough milk to form a soft dough.

Place dough on a well-floured board and pat into a circle, 3/4 inch thick. Using a 2 inch cookie cutter, cut out scones and place on greased baking sheet. Let rest for about 45 minutes in the refrigerator, uncovered.

Just before baking, beat egg in a small bowl with sugar; brush mixture on top of scones.

Bake 15-20 minutes or until golden brown. Makes about 12-15 scones.

MARLENE'S SCOTTISH GRANDMOTHER'S LEMON CURD TARTS

LEMON CURD

Grated rind of 3 lemons
Juice of 3 lemons
1 cup of sugar
3 eggs, well beaten
1/2 cup salted butter (1 stick)

Place rind and juice of lemons, sugar and butter in top of a double boiler. Cook, stirring frequently, until sugar is dissolved.

Add small amount of hot mix to the eggs and mix thoroughly. Return to double boiler and cook, stirring constantly until thick and smooth. Cool. Turn into a jar and cover. Store in refrigerator.

TART PASTRY

Use recipe for your favorite pie crust. Use fluted cutter and cut pastry into circles to line shallow English jam tart pans. With tines of a fork make holes in the pastry so it will not puff during baking. Bake at 425 degrees until tarts are very lightly browned, about 10 minutes. Remove pans to a cooling rack and cool tart shells in the pan to retain their shape. Fill with lemon curd as close to serving time as possible.

LEMON POPPY SEED CAKE

1 package Duncan Hines Lemon Supreme Cake Mix
3 eggs
1/3 cup vegetable oil
1 1/3 cups water
2 teaspoons grated lemon rind
1/4 cup poppy seeds
4 fresh lemons
1/3 cup granulated sugar

Spray Bundt pan with Baker's Joy. Prepare cake mix according to package directions adding vegetable oil, water and eggs. Add 2 teaspoons grated lemon rind and the poppy seeds to the mixture. Bake according to directions for Bundt pan.

Prepare mixture of 1/3 cup of freshly squeezed lemon juice and 1/3 cup of sugar. Stir until sugar is dissolved.

When cake is removed from the pan, use pastry brush to coat cake with glaze until all glaze is absorbed by the cake. Decorate cake with thinly sliced lemons.

Tea In France

My friend Judi Culbertson brought me *The Art of Tea* published by Mariage Frères as a souvenir from Paris several years ago. I read it and was intrigued by the differences between English and French teas. My husband and I had planned a trip to the Atlantic coast of France for several years. We love the south of France and would return there again and again, but felt we should see what the Atlantic Coast was like. I also wanted to explore the coastal village of Fécamp in Normandy where my mother's ancestors had come from several generations ago. We made an agreement that our trip would be an exploration of tearooms and beaches to satisfy both our interests.

As we began exploring the great beach resorts of the Atlantic Coast, including Deauville, Trouville, Honfleur, and Dinard we discovered that they had reached their height of fashion at the turn of the century. They were fashionable resorts when tea was also at its height of popularity. In town after town, we would see signs saying "salon de thé" on buildings, in hotels, and on sidewalk cafes. The only problem was that no one was drinking tea; everyone was drinking wine, aperitifs, mineral water or coffee. My interest was then piqued as to these ghosts of tearooms. I was frustrated as I could not speak French, and for the first two weeks of our trip, especially in the very small beach towns, virtually no one spoke English. I could not ask my questions about tea and the tearooms and could only contemplate the question in my own mind. In our dowager hotel in Dinard there was a very formal tearoom with dark velvet furniture, and heavy draperies covering the windows. The tea menu offered an extensive selection of loose teas. I wondered if anyone ever drank tea there. In the two days we spent at the hotel, I only saw people having alcoholic drinks. What impressed me most about this tearoom was the fact that there was an extra charge if you had milk, lemon or sugar in your tea. I guess it makes sense to charge extra for these things, but it was just such a different notion, as I could not imagine a restaurant in the United States charging for milk or sugar.

It was not until Paris, and my trip to the Mariage Frères tearoom, that I was finally able to ask my questions about French tea. Our waiter spoke English and had an uncle who lived in Manhattan. He very much wanted to open a tea salon in New York, and I really do expect to hear from him some day. He thought we might be partners in the venture. It was he who explained the art of French tea to me. He also told me that in the past tea had been considered the drink of invalids and old women; but that lately, it was beginning to become fashionable as it was around the turn of the century. He showed me how tea was brewed with the "tea sock". The teapot was preheated with boiling water. Then the loose tea was placed in a cotton filter suspended over the rim of the teapot. Boiling water was poured over the tea leaves, and after the tea had steeped for three to five minutes, the entire sock was removed from the teapot. There are separate socks for green, black, and flavored teas. A metal insulator was then put around the teapot to serve the same function as an English tea cozy.

It was amazing to me that the French took more care in brewing tea than the English, who do not worry about leaving the tea leaves in the pot to stew and make the tea bitter. This technique is similar to using a bouquet garni, often used in French cooking, in which spices are put into a small cheesecloth bag and later removed from the sauce or stew at the desired time. My waiter also told me that Mariage Frères would not sell their tea to anyone else in Paris as they would not brew it properly.

I guess it should not be a surprise to me that the French are so particular in brewing tea, as they raise all food preparation to the level of art. In fact, Mariage Frères calls their book *The Art of Tea*. Sugar at Mariage Frères was granulated and served with a sugar spade. This was the only place in France that I saw granulated sugar being served. At all other places, you received a large lump of sugar wrapped in paper. Either you used the whole thing, or broke it in half. No other choice was possible. At Mariage Frères, you could use the exact amount of sugar you desired. This was just another example of the care taken in serving the tea.

The food served along with the tea was another experience. For sandwiches, there was smoked salmon with cream cheese, cucumber with crème fraîche (open face sandwiches with the cucumber seeds cut out and the slices cut in quarters), foie gras on white bread, tuna spread very thinly on buttered bread and thin little squares of bread with a seasoned cheese like Boursin. In the center of the plate was a croque monsieur. This one had smoked salmon in the center and broiled cheese on top. It was cut with a circular pastry cutter and was absolutely delicious. It was very different from those I had in French sidewalk cafes as the fast food of Paris.

The next course served was pastries. Rather than the traditional fruit tarts, I wanted something I had never eaten before. I chose madeleines that were served with butter and tea jellies. One was Earl Grey tea jelly and the other was South African Red tea jelly which had a strong vanilla scent. I was very surprised that the madeleine tasted like a muffin; it was not like the sweet madeleines that Monet served his artist friends at Giverny at teatime and I had in the United States. The butter and jellies were the perfect complement to this type of madeleine. My last choice was a financier. This was a small cake made in the shape of a miniature pound cake. It was made with almond paste and green tea, which accounted for its unusual green color. My waiter told me that it was called a financier because it is rich in calories and expensive to make. This tea experience was probably the finest I had anywhere in the world. I was very impressed with the tea and especially the food.

People ask me what makes French tea different from English tea, and I tell them it is the food; not only the pastries, but the savories as well. In a recent series of French tea cooking classes that I held, my students told me that they like French tea much better than English tea. I think that is because the range of foods is so vast. When I began putting together recipes for my classes, I found myself going to Julia Child again and again. I remember buying *Mastering the Art of French Cooking* as a new bride anxious to make the recipes, but I found them extremely difficult and cumbersome and considered Julia too much of a perfectionist to emulate. It is only now after 23 years of cooking that I realize how wonderful her recipes are, and I am now capable of making them.

In putting together the recipes for this French Impressionist Tea Menu, I have included elements from the Mariage Frères tea, Claude Monet's recipes as recorded in his cooking journals by Claire Joyes in *Monet's Table*, recipes from Julia Child, and my own travel experiences. I have made all of these recipes many times and people have enjoyed them over the years. Dan and I discovered Gâteau a la Basque on a trip to St. Jean de Luz when we were staying in Biarritz. St. Jean de Luz was about a half hour drive south of Biarritz. After studying salons de thé and the beach at Biarritz we decided to go to St. Jean de Luz for dinner one evening. As luck would have it, it just so happened that evening the "T-Toro" Fete was being held. There were Basque bands playing in the streets and parades and dancing. We bought wonderful berets for our nieces Alix and Jessica. After roaming the streets for a while we finally found out that "T-Toro" had nothing to do with bulls, but was a fish soup which was very much like bouillabaisse. All of the restaurants in town featured a special T-Toro. We chose one that served "T-Toro with four fishes".

It was excellent, but the highlight of the meal was Gâteau à la Basque. This was a wonderful double crust sweet pastry tart with a custard filling. The top was sprinkled with granulated sugar. It was probably the best desert we had in all of France. When Dan and I returned to Biarritz that evening, there was a beautiful full moon and we decided to walk to the ocean. The bakeries were open very late at night, and we saw Gâteau à la Basque in a bakery window. We bought a whole gâteau and decided we would have it for breakfast the next morning. We did, and later ate it for snacks in the car on our way to the caves of Lascaux. I was so happy to find a recipe in a cookbook when I returned home; however, when I made it, I was not happy with the custard. The next time I substituted Julia Child's crème pâtissière and it came out just as I remembered it.

The suggestion for Benedictine liquor in the French Impressionist Tea Menu comes from our visit to Fécamp, the birthplace of my ancestors. The Benedictine distillery is the major source of income for the town and has made it world famous. When touring the distillery, we were shown many of the spices and herbs that go into the drink. One of the ingredients was tea! I felt my connection to the study of tea grow even deeper.

The French have given us a great legacy in regard to tea. Tea was introduced in France in 1648, ten years before England. A famous French doctor labeled it the "impertinent novelty of the century". The French were the first in Europe to make reference to putting milk in their tea. In 1680 in a letter Madame de la Sablière refers to taking tea with milk. The French introduced the rim in the center of the tea saucer to keep the cup from sliding. Madame Pompadour became a patroness of the Sèvres porcelain factory near Versailles and encouraged the development of fine porcelain that raised tea drinking to a higher art. The French introduced the thé dasant and the tango tea to Europe. In Biarritz and on the Riviera, people met to dance and drink tea every day. French tango dancers went to London to teach this new dance. The French designed the clipper ships that cut the time it took for tea to reach Europe. Proust raised the madeleine to a French tea time institution in his ode to the madeleine in Swann's Way. But most of all, the French gave tea a sense of high style that made it fashionable among the rich and famous. The level of food, flower arrangements, china, and porcelain contributed to a sophistication far beyond the homey, English teas. The introduction of the "tea sock" raises the quality of tea brewing and prevents the bitterness of the tea.

The popularity of French tea in New York continues to rise. It is very difficult to get Mariage Frères tea in New York. The T Salon and Dean and DeLuca are very often out of it. I buy my favorite, Marco Polo, whenever I see it as it is often out of stock. When I did my first French tea lecture at the Bayport-Blue Point library in May of 1996, I just assumed that I would serve Marco Polo tea. When I found out that it was $65 a pound, I thought I had made a big mistake in promising this tea at the lecture. I went ahead anyway, told the people what an expensive tea they were about to have and brewed it for the first time using the tea sock. They absolutely loved the tea, felt it was better than any English tea they had ever had, and felt privileged to be able to share the experience. It was like drinking an expensive champagne. With it I served Monet's Madeleines Au Citron from the same turn of the century recipe he used at Giverny. Everyone loved them.

Another important French legacy to tea is the impressionist artist notion of tea in the garden. The impressionists sought to capture the light and paint their subjects in ordinary surroundings. For years I have poured over French impressionist paintings with ladies drinking tea among their flowers. Tea should not only be taken in the winter indoors, but should be taken outside also in the nice weather. Dan and I have an 1873 Victorian home which is contemporaneous with Giverny and one of our greatest summer joys is sharing tea on the porch or in the garden with friends on a summer afternoon. As I sat writing this chapter on my porch, I was interrupted several times when friends stopped for tea. They know not to come by before four o'clock though. But at four, it is tea time, time to stop and regroup. Enough writing has been done for the day.

Claude Monet had tea daily at Giverny. When he invited friends from Paris or other parts of France, they would have lunch at 11:30 and then view the paintings and engage in much conversation. Tea was served under the lime trees, on the balcony, or near the pond. He served Ceylon, Darjeeling or China teas. When I serve tea on our porch or in our gardens from the replica of the very teapot Monet designed, eat madeleines made from his recipe, and enjoy the irises, roses, or nasturtiums that he surrounded himself with, I feel transported back to that time. I have even made his banana ice cream which I served at a tea/ice cream social. We froze it in a hand cranked freezer as he would have used then. It was wonderful. We added homemade hot fudge and I do not think I have ever had a better ice cream.

I continue to be fascinated by the French service of tea. When I came back to the United States, having been frustrated at not being able to ask questions in French about the tea service there, a French friend who is an artist explained to me that the French are very meticulous about food service and about tea. They do not want to have tea leaves floating in their cup. She told me that they sell cotton tea bags in the grocery stores and loose tea leaves are placed in these bags. When a friend at work, Alice Scuderi, told me she was going to Paris for a few weeks and asked if I wanted her to bring me anything back as a souvenir, I immediately asked her to bring me some of these cotton bags. Other friends had asked for perfume or silk scarves; I was happy she had an apartment and would be visiting the supermarket.

My friend Marion Cohn recently traveled to Paris with her husband and sons. She loved shopping for tea at Fauchon and brought back several varieties of loose tea. She brought a French apple tea to the First Bloom Tea in the Rose Garden at Meadow Croft this June (we usually serve Rose tea from Le Cordon Bleu, another excellent French tea). One of the ladies at our table chose this apple tea for us. I usually do not like apple teas as they are sweet and have a lot of cinnamon. I delayed having the tea, thinking we would choose another type later. I finally decided to try the tea. It had sat in the pot at least twenty minutes. I was amazed to find that not only did it not taste like apples and cinnamon, but that it was not bitter even though the leaves had remained in the pot so long. Another secret of French tea!

Marion also brought back Fauchon's house blend to try. It is a mix of lemon, orange, vanilla and lavender. It was wonderful. My friend Heidi Rosenau who works at the National Academy of Design in Manhattan and is a very serious connoisseur of tea is going to Paris and Russia this summer. I asked her to bring me back two more tea socks from Mariage Frères, as the ones I had gotten in New York were not of the same quality. I can't wait for Heidi's return so she can tell me of her Parisian tea adventures and those of Russia also.

A French Impressionist Tea

To be served in the garden in the late afternoon light

~ ~ ~

Pissaladaière Nicoise*

Croque Monsieur*

Pâté Sandwiches

Open face slices of white bread with Boursin cheese
Camembert Cheese wedges

Scones with Crème Fraîche and French preserves or
tea jelly

Fresh fruit tart*

Madeleines

Gâteau à la Basque*

Marco Polo Tea from Mariage Frères

Benedictine liquor

~ ~ ~

To be served on Limoge china or other French
tableware

*Recipes may be found on the following pages.

PISSALADIÈRE NICOISE

This is not a quiche, properly speaking, because it contains no eggs. In Nice it is made either in a pastry shell or on a flat round of bread dough like the Italian pizza.

2 lbs. minced onions
4 tablespoons olive oil
1 herb bouquet (4 parsley sprigs, 1/4 teaspoon thyme
    and 1/2 bay leaf tied in washed cheesecloth)
2 cloves unpeeled garlic
1/2 teaspoon salt
1 pinch of powdered cloves
1/8 teaspoon pepper
8 inch partially cooked pastry shell on a baking sheet
8 canned anchovy filets
16 pitted black olives (the dry Mediterranean type)
1 tablespoon olive oil

Cook the onions very slowly in the olive oil with the herb bouquet, garlic and salt for about one hour, or until very tender. Discard herb bouquet and garlic. Stir in cloves and pepper, and taste carefully for seasoning.

Preheat oven to 400 degrees.

Spread the onions in the pastry shell. Arrange anchovy filets over it in a fan-shaped design. Place the olives at decorative intervals. Drizzle on the oil. Bake in upper third of the preheated oven for 10 to 15 minutes, or until bubbling hot.

CROQUE MONSIEUR

For each sandwich:

2 slices of firm, white bread such as Pepperidge
　Farm or Arnold
2 thin slices of Swiss cheese
1 thin slice of boiled ham
1 egg mixed with 1/4 cup milk beaten well (mixture
　may be used for more than one sandwich)
Three inch crimped cookie cutter
Teflon coated frying pan
Shredded or chopped Swiss cheese

Place one slice of Swiss cheese, then one of ham,
then another of Swiss cheese between 2 slices of
bread. Pre-heat frying pan. Just lightly dip both sides
of bread in the egg-milk mixture. Do not soak bread.
Then lightly brown on both sides; Swiss cheese
should be melted. You may have to press with a
spatula. Then cut sandwich with cookie cutter. Put
some of the shredded or chopped cheese on top of the
sandwich and put under broiler until just bubbling.
Serve immediately.

FRESH FRUIT TART

Fruit tarts can be made from any fruit that is in season or is available and is perfect and unblemished. Strawberries, raspberries, or other fruit or combinations of fruit can be arranged in a pleasing pattern over a bed of pastry cream in a tart shell and then glazed.

For a strawberry tart, choose enough strawberries that are perfect and wash them in a colander. Cut off just the stem and hull them, leaving the whole berry intact. Make the tart shell and Crème Pâtissière as directed below. Paint the interior of the tart shell with the glaze using a pastry brush. Fill with the Crème Pâtissière and start placing the strawberries, stem end down, around the outside perimeter of the tart shell. Try to have strawberries of the same size. Continue placing them in concentric circles with the strawberries touching on their sides. Continue until you reach the center to place the last strawberry. Paint with glaze. The results are spectacular and people will be awed by this beautiful desert.

I always make my pastry in a Cuisinart to ensure that the shortening and flour are mixed evenly and to prevent the butter from becoming warm. Even the warmth of your hands can affect the pastry. Also, it is imperative to keep all the ingredients very cold, especially the butter and the water. If you are not a purist and want to save time and trouble, the Pillsbury pie crusts in the refrigerator section of your supermarket are excellent and some of the best cooks I know use them. I use them in my cooking classes and students are amazed at how good the crusts taste. They are convenient, easy to work with and are tender and flaky. If you want to make your own tart shell, you can use the recipe below.

Pastry Recipe (for an 8" shell)

1 3/4 cups Hecker's unbleached flour
1 teaspoon salt
12 tablespoons chilled butter (salted or unsalted)
Ice water

Place dry ingredients in bowl of food processor with steel blade. Pulse several times to mix dry ingredients. Then add butter and pulse until mixture resembles a course meal and all of the butter is distributed equally. Add 5 tablespoons of ice water or more if necessary until dough begins to mass around the blade and then clears the sides of the food processor. Roll out as you would a pie shell and place it in a fluted tart pan with removable bottom. Cut excess dough from top of tart pan by rolling over it with a rolling pin. Pierce all over with tines of fork. Place a sheet of aluminum foil weighted down with beans or pie weights in tart shell and bake for approximately 10 minutes at 425 degrees until lightly browned. Remove weights and foil and bake for an additional 5 minutes. Cool on wire rack.

GÂTEAU À LA BASQUE

PASTRY:

2 3/4 cups Hecker's unbleached flour
13 tablespoons butter cut into pieces
3/4 cup sugar
2 eggs beaten
1 tablespoon rum
1/2 cup apricot preserves, heated and strained
1 recipe Crème Pâtissière*
1 egg well beaten

Put the flour and sugar in a Cuisinart. Pulse a few times until the ingredients are mixed. Add pieces of butter and pulse until butter is evenly distributed. Add the eggs and rum and process until the dough just clears the sides of the bowl.

Divide the dough into 2 portions; 1/3 and 2/3 of dough. Chill for at least one hour. Roll out each portion. With the 2/3 portion line the bottom of a nine inch by two inch deep unfluted tart pan with removable bottom. Brush bottom of pan with strained, heated apricot preserves. Fill with Crème Pâtissière. Roll the remainder of the dough and place on top of the tart pan.

Trim and pinch edges of the dough together. Make a lattice pattern with the tines of a fork. Brush with beaten egg. Cook in 400 degree oven for approximately 35 minutes or until brown. Cool on rack. When cool, sprinkle with white granulated sugar.

*Crème Pâtissière recipe may be found on page 62.

61

CRÈME PÂTISSIÈRE

1 cup granulated sugar
5 egg yolks
Three quart mixing bowl
A wire whip or electric beater

2/3 cup sifted all-purpose flour
2 cups boiling milk
A clean even bottomed 2 1/2 quart enamel saucepan
A wire whip
1 tablespoon butter
1/2 tablespoon vanilla extract

Gradually beat the sugar into the egg yolks and continue beating for 2 to 3 minutes until the mixture is pale yellow and forms a ribbon. Beat in the flour. Beating the yolk mixture, gradually pour on the boiling milk in a thin stream of droplets.

Pour into saucepan and set over moderately high heat. Stir with wire whip, reaching all over bottom of pan. As the sauce comes to the boil, it will get lumpy, but will smooth out as you beat it. When boil is reached, beat over moderately low heat for 2 to 3 minutes to cook the flour. **Be careful custard does not scorch in bottom of pan**.

Remove from heat and beat in the butter and vanilla. If custard is not used immediately, clean it off the sides of the pan and dot top of custard with softened butter to prevent a skin from forming over the surface. Crème pâtissière will keep for a week under refrigeration or may be frozen.

Glaze:

1 cup red currant jelly
2 tablespoons granulated sugar
A pastry brush

Boil the currant jelly and sugar in a small saucepan until last drops from the spoon are sticky. Paint the interior of the shell with a thin coating of the glaze and allow to set for 5 minutes. This will give the shell a light waterproofing. Reserve the rest of the glaze for strawberries. Warm it briefly if it has hardened. Paint thin coating over strawberries with pastry brush when tart is assembled.

Where to Buy Loose Tea

Coffee Bean Supreme Ltd.
35 N. Main Street
Sayville, NY 11782
(516) 244-9543

Moore's Gourmet Market
225 Main Street
Port Jefferson, NY 11777
(516) 928-1443

Sedona Coffee & Tea
Main Street
Bridgehampton, NY 11932
(516) 537-5880

Kitchen Classics
Main Street
Bridgehampton, NY 11932
(516) 537-1111

Barefoot Contessa
46 Newtown Lane
East Hampton, NY
(516) 324-0240

Wild By Nature
198 Main Street
East Setauket, NY 11733
(516) 246-5500

Quiet Corner Cafe
134 Main Street
Port Jefferson, NY 11777
(516) 473-3311

Harney & Sons*
Village Green
P.O. Box 638
Salisbury, CT 06068
(800) Tea-Time

*Catalaog available for mail orders.

Where to Buy Loose Tea

DEAN AND DELUCA*
560 Broadway
New York, NY 10012
(800) 221-7714
Mariage Frères available here.

Porto Rico Importing Co.*
201 Bleeker St.
New York, NY 10012
(800) 453-5908

Charleston Tea Plantation, Inc.*
6617 Maybank Highway
P.O. Box 12810
Charleston, SC 29422
(800) 443-5987

Murchie's Tea and Coffee Ltd.*
5580 Parkwood Way
Richmond, British Columbia
Canada V6V 2M4
(800) 663-0400

Flash in the Pan
49 Main Street
Sayville, NY 11782
(516) 563-8585

Babylon Bean
17 Fire Island Avenue
Babylon, NY 11702
(516) 587-7729

*Catalog available for mail orders.

Where to Buy Clotted Cream

Quiet Corner Cafe
134 Main Street
Port Jefferson, NY 11777
(516) 473-3311

La Bonne Quiche
407 Fort Salonga Rd.
Northport, NY 11768
(800) 561-6601

Wild By Nature
198 Main Street
East Setauket, NY 11733
(516) 246-5500

DEAN AND DELUCA
560 Broadway
New York, NY 10012
(800) 221-7714

Macy's Herald Square
151 W. 34th St.
New York, NY 10001
(212) 695-4400

Wolferman's*
One Muffin Lane
P.O. Box 15913
Shawnee Mission, KS 66285
(800) 999-1910

Village Cheese Shop
11 Main St.
Southampton, NY 11968
(516) 283-6949

*Catalog available for mail orders.

Resources

Antique Costume & Prop Rental
709 Main Street
Port Jefferson, NY 11777
(516) 331-2261
Nancy Altman Guzzetta
Vintage tea gowns, silver and other necessities for a proper tea.

Huntington Antiques Center
231 Wall Street
Huntington, NY 11742
(516) 549-0105
Katherine Stevens
Large tea caddy selection.

Meadow Croft
Suffolk County Parks Department
Middle Road
Sayville, NY 11782
Robert Gaffney, County Executive
(516) 854-4970

TEA A MAGAZINE
P.O. Box 348
Scotland, CT 06264
(203) 456-1145
Published bimonthly.

VICTORIA
P.O. Box 7115
Red Oak, IA 51591
(800) 876-8696
Magazine published monthly.

Reva Paul Special Orders
45 East 89th St.
New York, NY 10128
(212) 722-0486
Hand decorated sugars, mints and place cards.

Resources

The Charms of Tea Newsletter
P.O. Box 29029 - 55 Wyndham St. N.
Guelph, Ontario N1H 8J4
Canada
(519) 836-0620

Tea on Long Island

Rasberries
1026B Park Boulevard
Massapequa, NY 11762
(516) 797-1763

Afternoon tea from 3PM to 4:30PM Sunday through Friday
(closed on Saturday).

Greenport Tea Co., Inc.
119A Main Street
Greenport, NY 11944
(516) 477-8744

Tea served from 11AM to 5PM Wednesday, Thursday and
Sunday. Friday and Saturday tea served from 11AM to 6PM.
Closed Monday and Tuesday.

Garden City Hotel
45 Fifth Avenue
Garden City, NY 11530
(516) 747-3000

Tea served on Saturday only from 3PM to 5PM. Reservations
are required.

Tea Room at Stony Brook, Ltd.
97 E. Main Street
Stony Brook, NY 11790
(516) 751-1232

Call in advance and your tea will be ready for service. Tea
served seven days a week.

Quiet Corner Cafe
134 Main Street
Port Jefferson, NY 11777
(516) 473-3311

Tea served from 3PM till closing. Open seven days a week.

Tea on Long Island

The Silver Platter
451 Route 25A
Miller Place, NY 11764
(516) 473-3957

Call in advance for tea service as reservations are required.

Tea in New York City

Greenwich Village:
Tea & Sympathy
108 Greenwich Ave. (bet. 7th & 8th Aves.)
(212) 807-8329
Hours: Monday through Friday 11:30AM - 6PM
Saturday and Sunday 1PM - 6PM

Anglers & Writers
420 Hudson St. at St. Lukes Pl.
(212) 675-0810
Hours: 3PM - 7PM Daily

Fifth Avenue bet. 53rd and 63rd:
Felissimo
10 W. 56th St.
(212) 247-5656
Hours: Monday through Saturday 10AM - 6PM
Sunday 12 Noon - 5PM

Le Salon De Thé at Henri Bendel
712 Fifth Avenue
(212) 247-1100
Hours: 2:30PM - 5PM Daily

The Palm Court at the Plaza
768 Fifth Avenue
(212) 759-3000
Hours: Monday through Saturday 3:45PM - 6PM
Sunday 4PM - 6PM

The Pembroke Room at the Lowell
28 E. 63rd. St. bet. Park and Madison
(212) 838-1400
Hours: 3:30PM - 6:30PM Daily

Tea in New York City

Fifth Avenue bet. 53rd and 63rd (cont'd):
The Hotel Pierre
795 Fifth Ave. at 61st
(212) 838-8000
Hours: 3PM - 5:30PM Daily

Midtown:
The Peacock Alley at the Waldorf
301 Park Ave. bet. 49th and 50th
(212) 355-3000
Hours: Monday through Saturday 2PM - 5:30PM
Closed Sunday

The New York Palace Hotel
45 Madison Ave. bet. 50th and 51st
(212) 888-7000
Hours: 2PM - 6PM Daily

MacKenzie-Childs Ltd.
829 Madison Avenue
(212) 557-6050
Tea Served from 2PM to 6PM daily. A fun, fantasy experience.

Lincoln Center:
The Mayfair Lounge at the Mayfair
610 Park Avenue at 65th
(212) 288-0800
Hours: 3PM - 5:30PM Daily

Metropolitan Museum/Museum Mile:

The Museum Bar & Cafe at the Metropolitan Museum of Art
1000 Fifth Ave. at 82nd
(212) 535-7710
Hours: Tuesday, Wednesday, Thursday &Sunday 9:30AM -
9PM
Friday & Saturday 11:30AM - 4:30PM
Closed Monday

The Tea Salon at the Stanhope
995 Fifth Avenue bet. 80th and 81st
(212) 288-5800
Hours: 1PM - 5:30PM Daily

Metropolitan Museum/Museum Mile (cont'd):
Dean and Deluca Museum Cafe at the Guggenheim
1071 Fifth Avenue bet. 88th and 89th
(212) 423-3500
Hours: Sunday through Wednesday 8AM - 7PM
Thursday 8AM - 3PM
Friday & Saturday 8AM - 9PM
Closed Monday

Trois Jean
154 E. 79th St. bet. Lexington and Third
New York, NY
(212) 988-4858
Hours: Noon - 5:30PM Daily
For a wonderful French tea in America.

Tea in Florida

Disney's Grand Floridian Resort
Lake Buena Vista
Lake Buena Vista, FL
(407) 824-3000

Breakers Hotel
1 South Country Road
Palm Beach, FL
(407) 659-8460

The Chesterfield Hotel
363 Coconut Row
Palm Beach, FL 33480
(407) 659-5800

Brazilian Court Hotel
301 Australian Ave.
Palm Beach, FL 33480
(407) 655-7740

Ritz Carlton
100 S. Ocean Blvd.
Manalapan, FL 33462
(407) 533-6000

Where to Buy Loose Tea in Florida:

C'est Si Bon Gormet Store
280 Sunset Ave.
Palm Beach, FL 33480
(407) 659-6503

Publix Market
265 Sunset Ave.
Palm Beach, FL 33480
(407) 655-4120

British Emporium
150 Worth Avenue
Palm Beach, FL 33480
(407) 853-0054
Includes a wide selection of china and other tea equippage.

Tea in London

Brown's Hotel
Albemarle Street
London W1

Claridge's
Brook Street
Mayfair, London W1

Maids of Honour
Newens 288 Kew Road
Kew Gardens, Richmond, Surrey

Ritz Hotel
Piccadilly, London W1

Waldorf Hotel
Aldwych, London WC2

The Pump House
Bath Street
Bath England

Where to Buy Loose Tea in London

Fortnum and Mason
181 Piccadilly
London W1

Harrods
Knightsbridge, London SW1

Twinings
216 The Strand
London WC2

Tea in Paris

Angelina
226 Rue de Rivoli
75001 Paris

Mariage Frères
30-32 Rue du Bourg-Tibourg
75004 Paris

Mariage Frères
13 Rue des Grands Augustins
75006 Paris

Hotel Ritz
15 Place Vendome
75001 Paris

Where to Buy Loose Tea in Paris

Fauchon
28 Place de la Madeleine
75008 Paris

Mariage Frères
30-32 Rue du Bourg-Tibourg
75004 Paris

Mariage Frères
13 Rue des Grands Augustins
75006 Paris

Verlet
26 Rue Saint-Honoré
75001 Paris

Reader's Suggestions

The Beverly Hilton Hotel
Beverly Hills, California (310) 274-7777
Linda Flor, Ventura, Califonia

Tottenham Court
242 East Ojai Avenue
Ojai, California (805) 646-2339
Linda Flor, Ventura, California

Four Seasons Biltmore Hotel
1260 Channel Drive
Santa Barbara, California (805) 969-2261
Linda Flor, Ventura, California

& Tea
28871 Agoura Rd.
Agoura Hills, California   (818) 889-3488
Linda Flor, Ventura, California

Hotel Del Coronado
1500 Orange Avenue
Coronado, California (619) 435-6611
Linda Flor, Ventura, California

Let's Get Cooking (School and Store)
Westlake Village, California
(818) 991-3940
Linda Flor, Ventura, California

Olde English Tea Room
3 Devotion Road
Scotland, Connecticut (203) 456-8651
Michele DeRubeis, Blue Point, New York

Ritz-Carlton, (downtown)
181 Peachtree Street, N.E.
Atlanta, Georgia (404) 659-0400
Sandy Schimpf, Bayport, New York

Sheraton Moana Surfrider
2365 Kalakaua Ave.
Honolulu, Hawaii (808) 922-3111
Diane Anderson, No. Babylon, New York

Reader's Suggestions

Princeville Hotel
Princeville, Kauai, Hawaii (808) 826-9644
Diane Anderson, No. Babylon, New York

Windsor Court Hotel
300 Gravier Street
New Orleans, Louisiana   (504) 523-6000
Doris Idoyaga, No. Babylon, New York

Special Teas
One Grafton Common
Grafton, Massachusetts (508) 839-7447
Joan Avato, South Grafton, Massachusetts

Victorian Rose Tea Room
30 West Jordan Street
Brevard, North Carolina (704) 883-3838
Ann Marie Roberts, Blue Point, New York

Gatelodge Restaurant
3229 NW Pittock Drive
Portland, Oregon   (503) 823-3627
Cathy Vail, Bayport , New York

British Tea Garden
725 S.W. Tenth Avenue
Portland, Oregon (503) 221-7817
Suzanne Johnson, Rocky Point, New York

The Heathman Hotel
1001 S.W. Broadway (at Salmon)
Portland, Oregon   (503) 241-4100
Cathy Vail, Bayport, New York

Rose Manor English Bed and Breakfast
124 South Linden Street
Manheim, Pennsylvania (717) 664-4932
Nancy Caccia, Bayshore, New York

Hotel Sorrento
900 Madison
Seattle, Washington (206) 622-6400
Linda Malanchuk Finan, Olympia, Washington

Reader's Suggestions

Southampton Princess Hotel
South Shore Road
Southampton Parish, Bermuda (809) 238-8000
Michele DeRubeis, Blue Point, New York

The Lighthouse Tea Room
Gibbs Hill Lighthouse
Lighthouse Rd. between South Shore and Middle Roads
Southampton Parish, Bermuda (809) 238-8679
Michele DeRubeis, Blue Point, New York

The Empress Hotel
721 Government Street
Victoria, British Columbia (604) 384-8111
Barbara Thuma, Bayport, New York

Murchie's
1200 Homer Street
Vancouver, British Columbia (604) 662-3776
Barbara Thuma, Bayport, New York
Catalog for loose tea (800) 663-0400

Selfridge's Department Store
400 Oxford Street
London, England Tel. 071/629-1234
Bette Beynon, Holbrook, New York

Insomnia Cafe
8164 Melrose Avenue
Los Angeles, California (213) 655-3960
Michael Walters, Los Angeles, California

Bourgeois Pig
5931 Franklin Avenue
Los Angeles, California (213) 962-6366
Michael Walters, Los Angeles, California

Ojai Coffee Roasting Co.
337 E. Ojai Avenue
Ojai, California (805) 646-4478
Linda Flor, Ventura, California

Bibliography

A Highland Seer, *Reading Tea-Leaves*, With an Introduction by James Norwood Pratt and an Afterword by John Harney. New York: Clarkson Potter, 1993.

Burgess, Anthony (Preface). *The Book of Tea*. Paris, France: Flammarion, 1992.

Easton, Ellen. *The Afternoon Tea Guide*. New York: Red Wagon Press, 1995.

Foley, Tricia. *Having Tea*. New York: Clarkson Potter, 1987.

Foley, Tricia. *Linens and Lace*. New York: Clarkson Potter, 1990.

Hewitt, William W. *Tea Leaf Reading*. St. Paul, MN: Llewellyn Publications, 1992.

Joyes, Claire. *Monet's Table, The Cooking Journals of Claude Monet*. New York: Simon and Schuster, 1989.

Leaf, Alexandra. *The Impressionists' Table; Recipes and Gastronomy of 19th Century France*. New York: Rizzoli, 1994.

Manchester, Carole. *French Tea*. New York: The Hearst Corporation, 1993.

The Meriden Britannia Co., *The Meriden Britannia Silver-Plate Treasury*, New York: Dover Publications, 1982.

Niles, Bo and McNiff, Veronica. *The New York Book of Tea, Where to take Tea and Buy Tea and Teaware*. New York: City and Company, 1995.

Pettigrew, Jane, Editor, *Guild of Tea Shops, The Definitive Guide to the Best Tea Places in Britain,* The Tea Council Ltd., 1996.

Pettigrew, Jane, *The National Trust Book of Tea-Time Recipes,* The National Trust, London, 1991.

Pickford, Ian, *Pocket Edition, Jackson's Hallmarks*, Antique Collectors' Club Ltd, Woodbridge, England, 1991.

Pratt, James Norwood. *The Tea Lover's Treasury*. San Ramon, CA: 101 Productions, Ortho Information Services,1982.

Smith, Michael. *The Afternoon Tea Book*. New York: Collier Books, Macmillan Publishing Company, 1986.

Victoria. *The Charms of Tea, Reminiscences and Recipes*. New York: The Hearst Corporation, 1991.

READERS SUGGESTION FORM

Because resources are ever changing, I would appreciate any comments you may have relevant to an unlisted or new resouce that you may be aware of. Although I will attempt to include this information in future publications, space may not allow all entries. I thank you in advance for your input. Please use the space below for your comments and return to Carole Pichney, P.O. Box 944, Bayport, NY 11705.

(Please print)

NAME_____

ADDRESS_____

CITY/STATE_____

PHONE_____

• •

For additional copies of *How to Serve a Proper Victorian Tea*, send a check or money order for the special introductory rate of $15.00 which includes shipping and handling made payable to:

Carole Pichney
P. O. Box 944
Bayport, NY 11705

Please include a photocopy of this form and allow 2 to 4 weeks for delivery.

• •

(Please Print Clearly)

Name_____

Address_____

City/State/Zip_____

Daytime Phone_____

If you would like your copy of the book autographed, please check here _____ and indicate below how you would like the autograph to read.

• •

~ About the Author ~

Carole Pichney has made presentations on period teas at museums, historical societies, community education programs and libraries in the New York Metropolitan area. She has traveled extensively in England, France and the United States researching tea, china, antique silver and period recipes. She has given cooking lessons and coordinated teas and demonstrations for many organizations. She lives with her husband Dan in an 1873 Victorian home in Bayport Long Island that they have been restoring over the last 15 years.

Requests for information on Carole's availability for speeches, seminars and consulting should be directed to her at P.O. Box 944, Bayport, New York 11705.